AF480518
Ant
Bear
Cat
Dog
Elephant
Quail
Raccoon
Snake
Turtle
Unicorn
Vulture
Walrus
X-Ray Fish
Yak
Zebra
This Book Belongs to :
Name : ________________
Age : ________________

Are You readY
to discover
AlPhabet
with Animals!
Let's GO
Vulture
Walrus
X-Ray Fish
Yak
Zebra

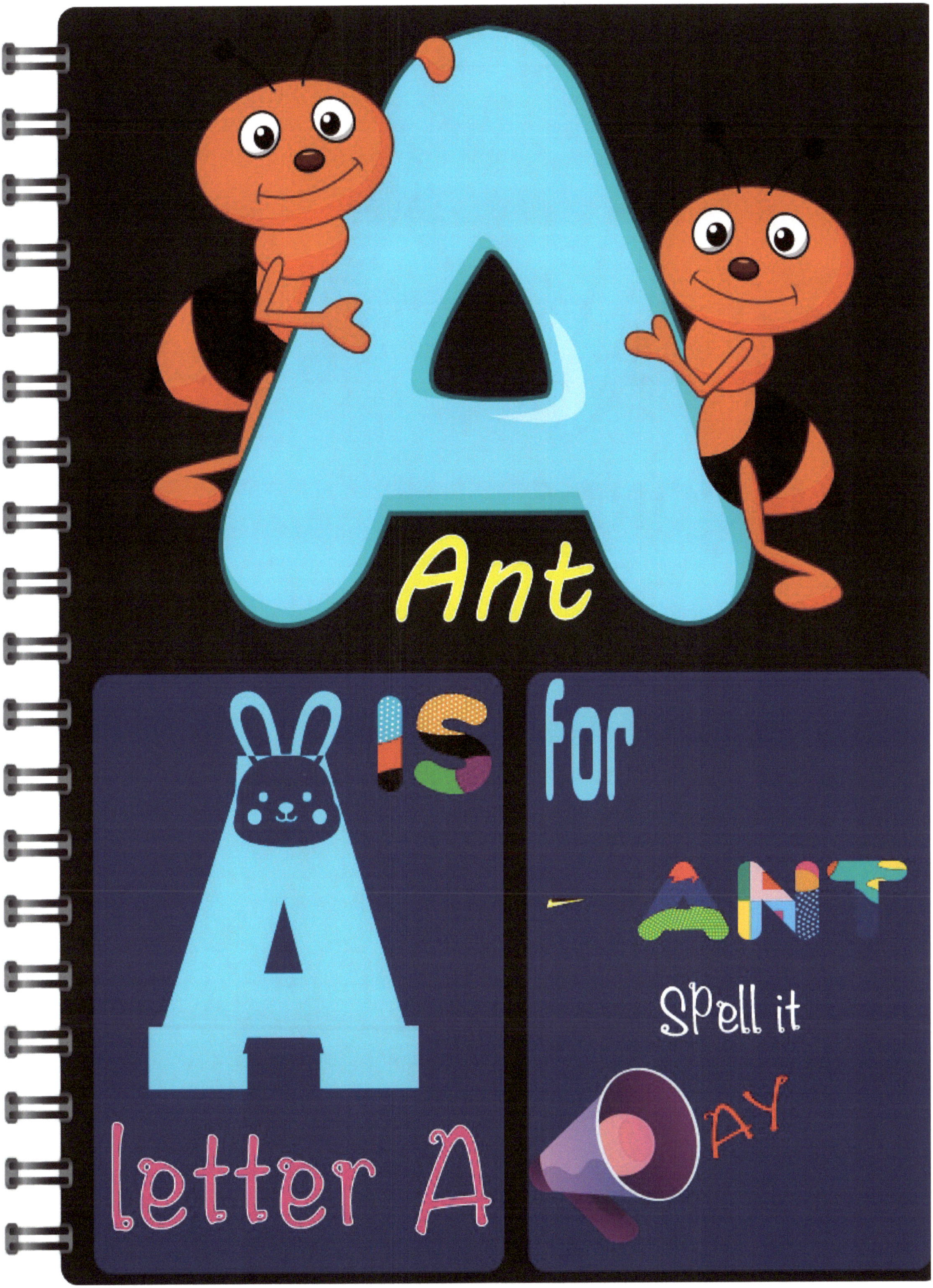

A

Ant

is for

letter A

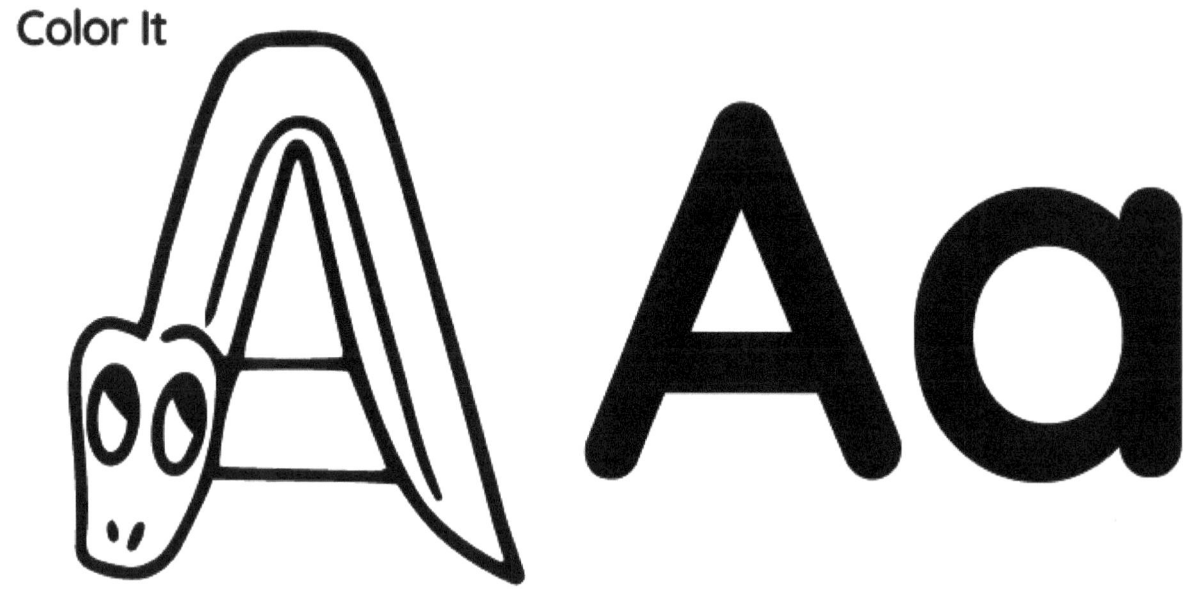

ANACONDA

Trace it

A

a

Anaconda

B
Bear

B is for
letter B
BEAR
Spell it
BEE

Bd

BUTTERFLY

B

b

Butterfly

Cat

's
letter C

for
CAT
spell it
CEE

Color It

CAT

Trace it

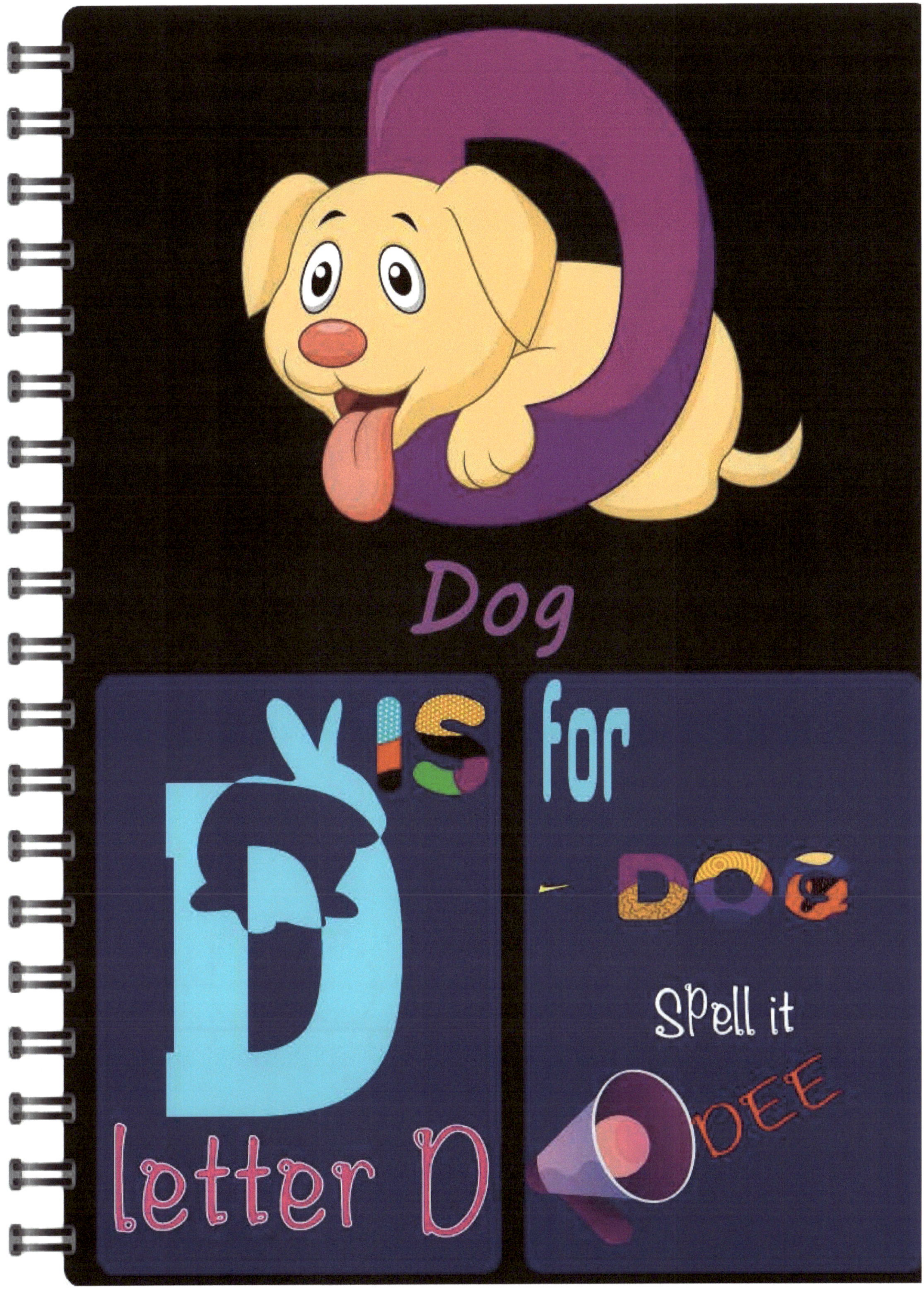
Dog
D IS for
DOG
Spell it
DEE
letter D

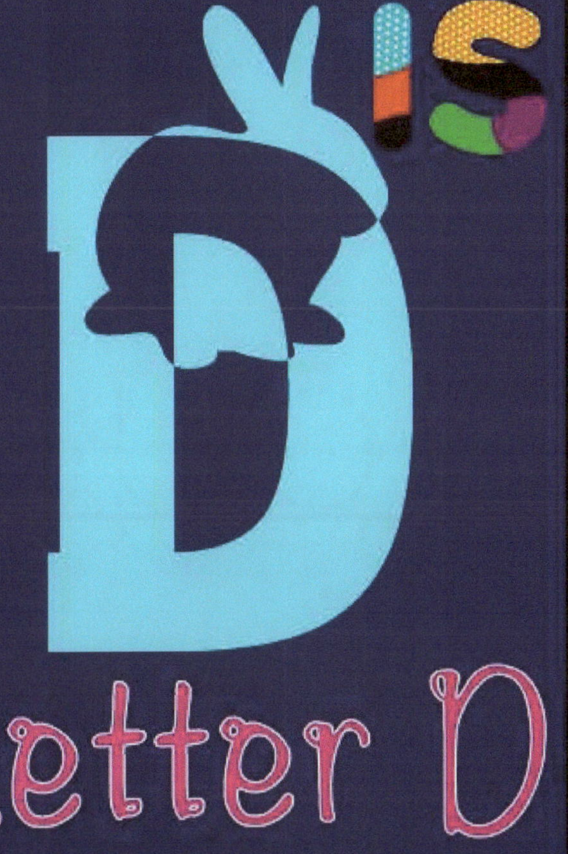

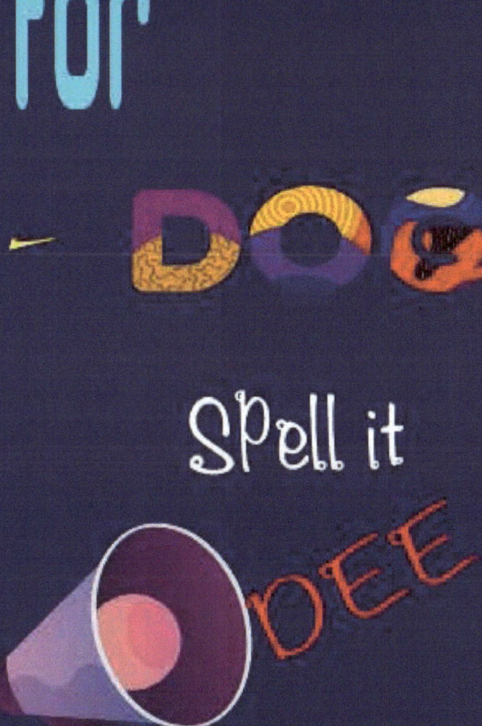

Dd

D

d

Elephant

Color It

ELEPHANT

Trace it

E

e

Elephant

is for

FISH

Spell it

EEF

letter F

Ff

F

f

Fly Fly Fly

Giraffe

G is for
GIRAFFE
Spell it
GDJY
letter G

Goose

Gg

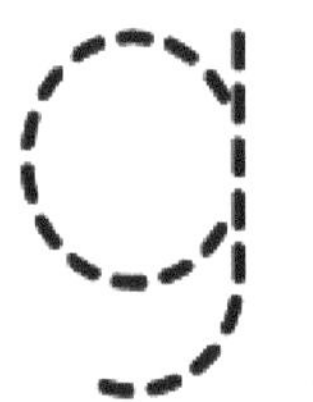

Horse

is for

HORSE

Spell it

letter H

HATCH

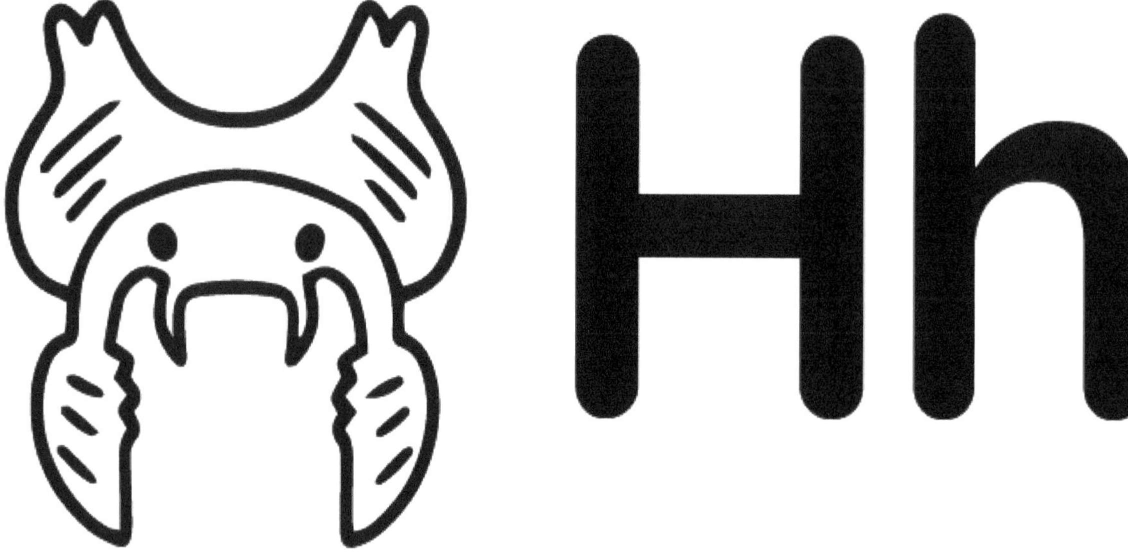

HERMIT CRAB

H

h

Hermitcrab

Iguana
is for
IGUANA
spell it
Spell it
letter I

Color It

INSECT

Ii

Trace it

Insect

Jaguar
is for
JAGUAR
Spell it
DJAY
letter J

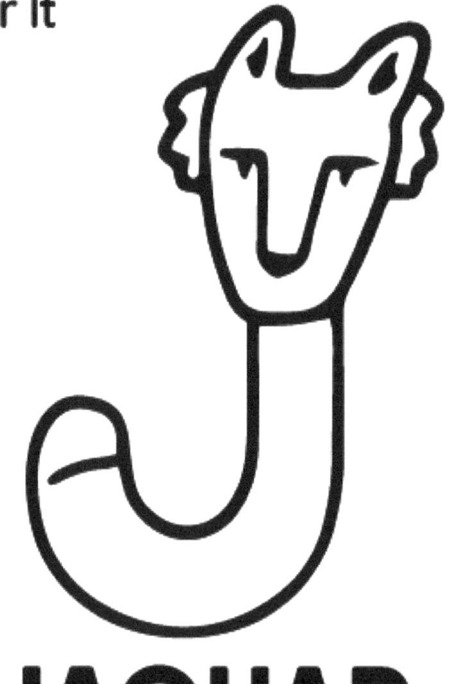

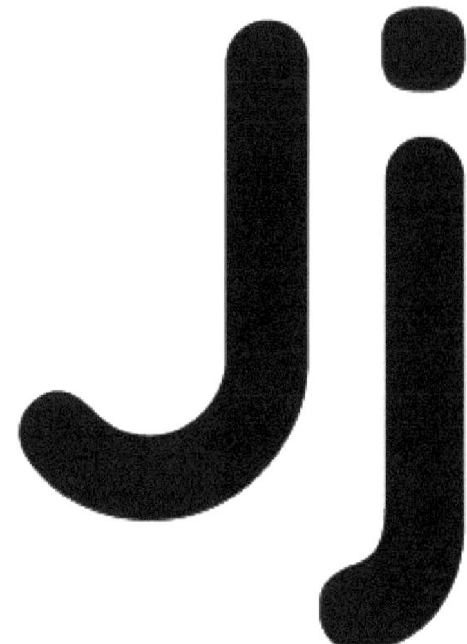

Trace it

Koala
is for
KOALA
Spell it
OKAY
letter K

Kk

KANGAROO

K

k

Kangaroo

Lion
is for
- LION
Spell it
ELL
Letter L

LI

L

I

Lizard

Monkey
M is for
- MONKEY
Spell it
EMM
letter M

MOTH

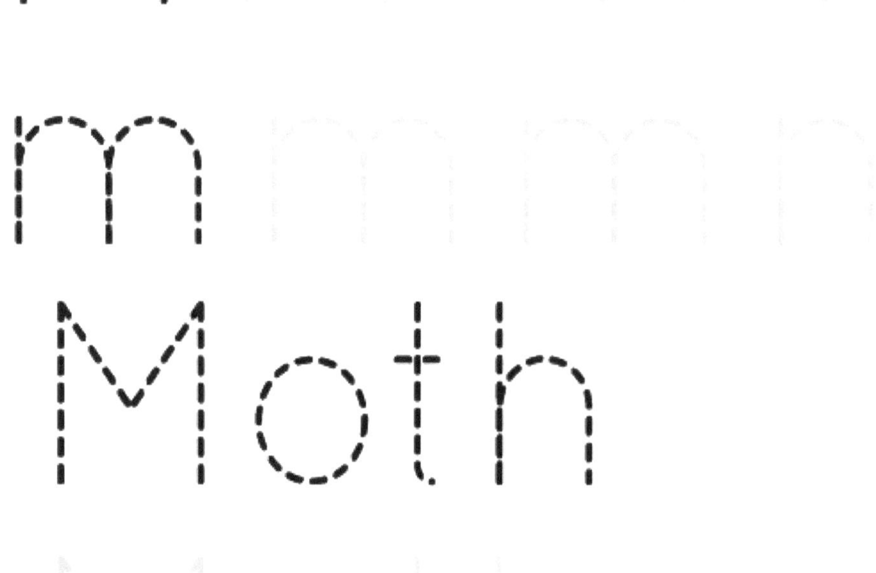

Narwhal

IS for

- NARWHAL

Spell it

NENN

letter N

NUMBAT

Nn

N

n

Numbat

Owl
is for
Owl
letter O
Spell it
ow

OCELOT

Penguin

P **IS** for

Spell it

letter p

Color It

Pp

PIG

Trace it

P

p

Pig Pig Pig

Quail

Q is for

letter Q

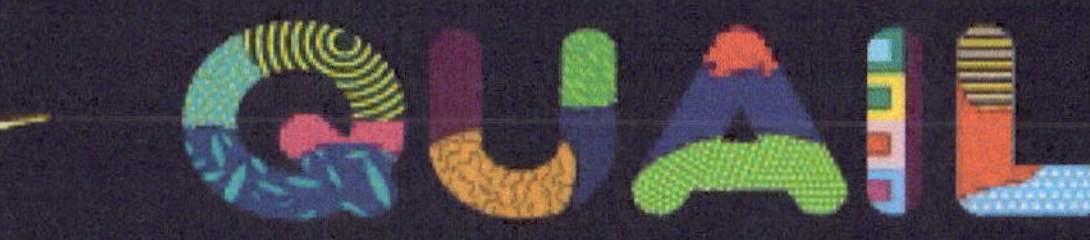

Spell it

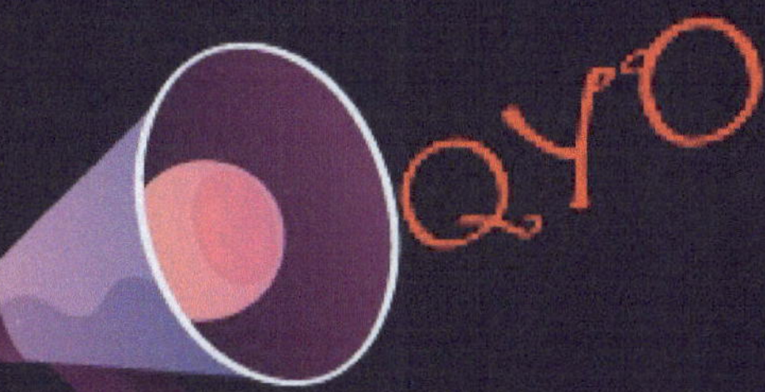

Color It

QUAIL

Trace it

Quail

Raccoon
R is for
- RACCOON
Spell it
ARR
letter R

RABBIT

Rr

R

r

Rabbit

Snake

is for

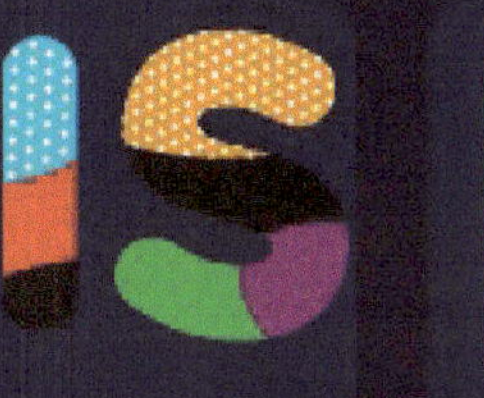

letter S

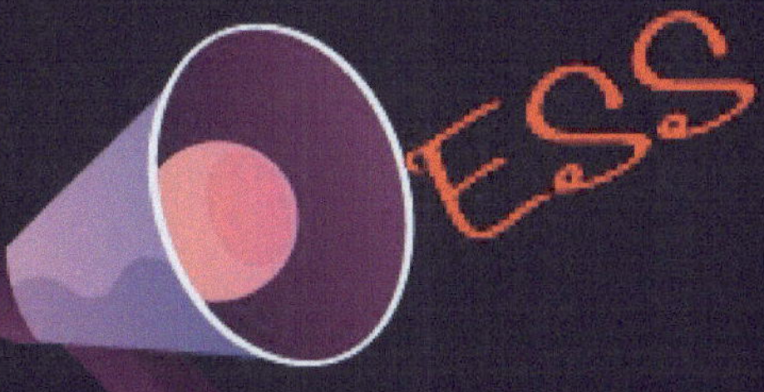

Ss

S

s

Turtle

T is for

TURTLE

Spell it

TEE

letter T

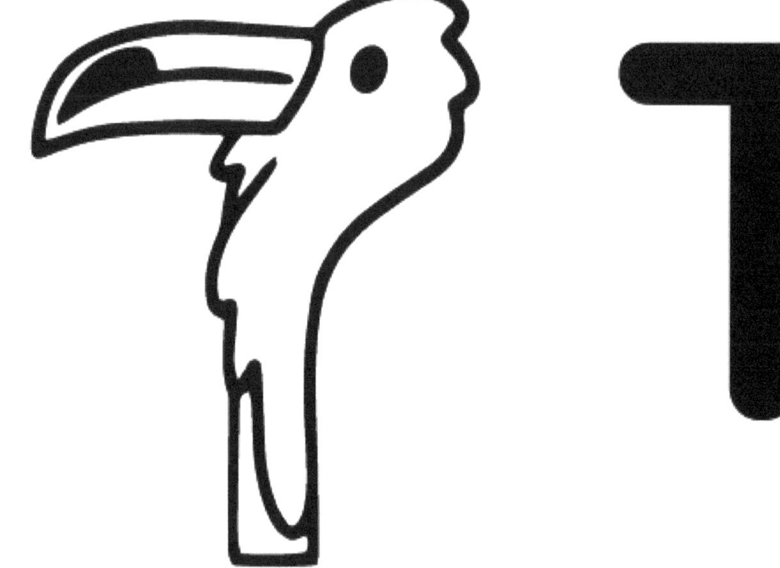

TUCAN

UNICORN
Spell it

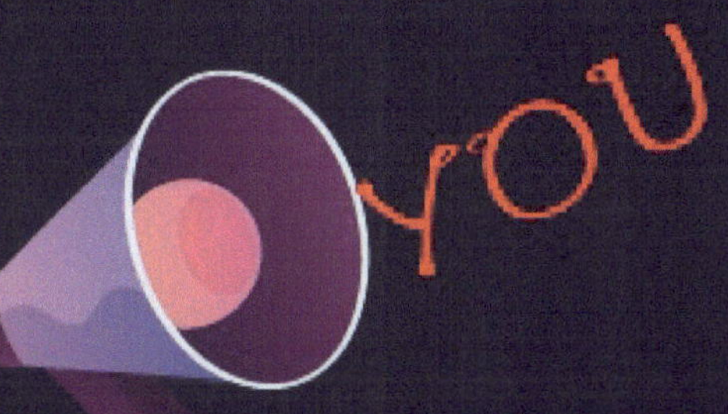

URCHIN

U u

U U U U U U U

U U U U U U U U

Urchin

Urchin

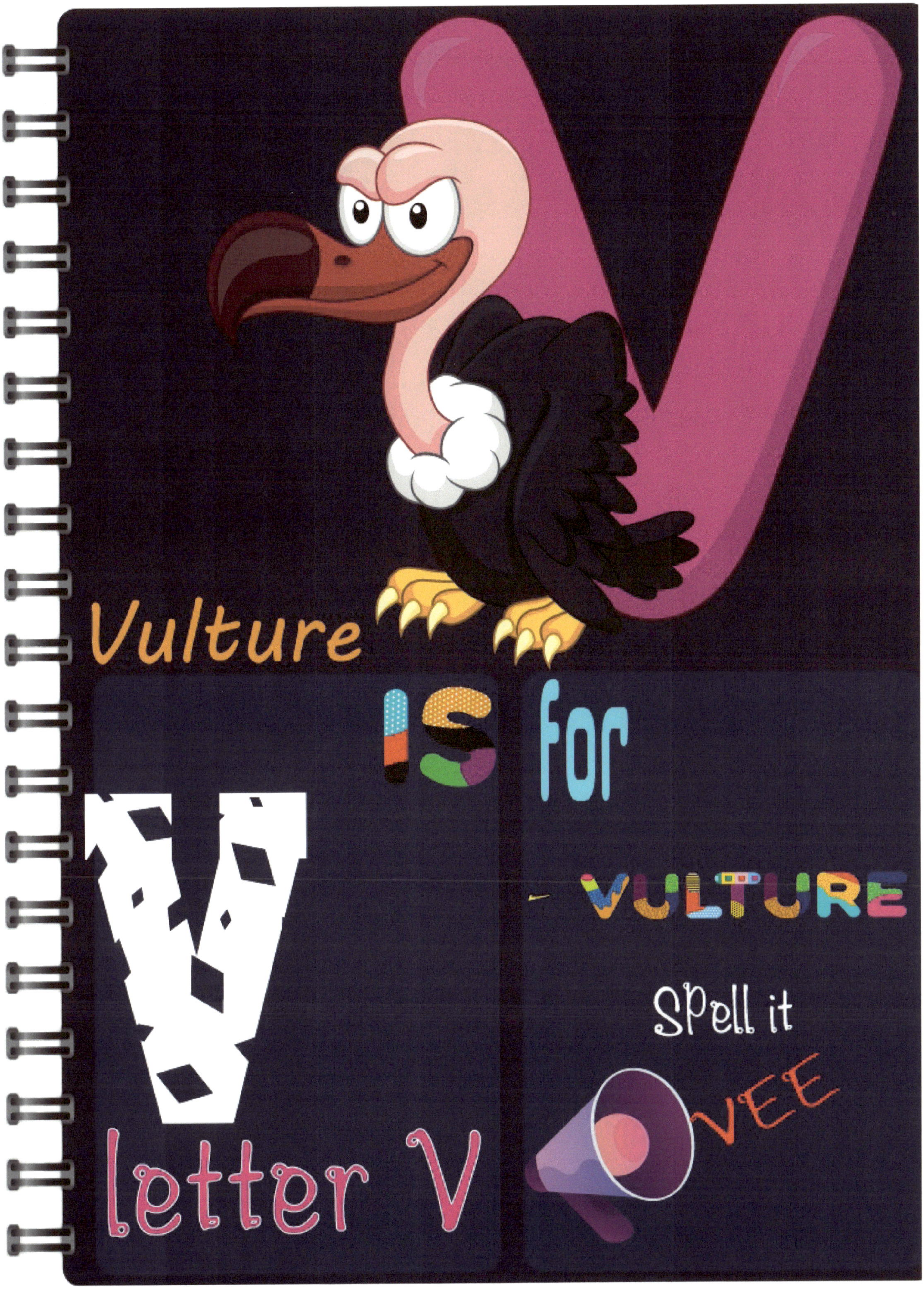

Vulture
IS for
letter V
- VULTURE
Spell it
VEE

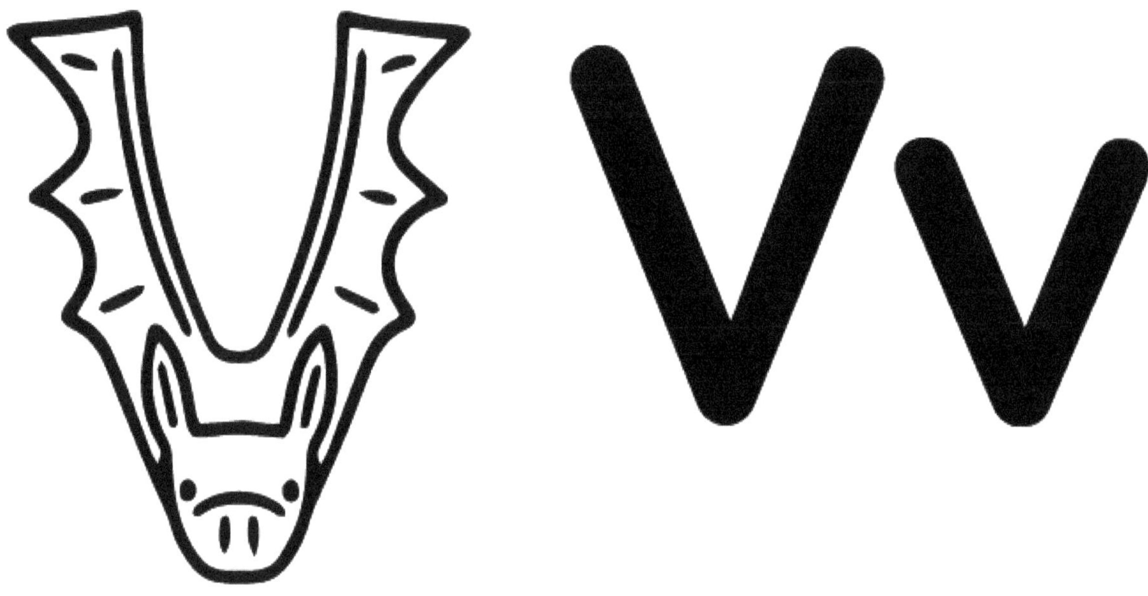

VAMPIRE BAT

V
v
Vampire bat

Walrus

W is for

WALRUS

Spell it

DOUBLE V

letter W

Color It

Ww
WORM

Trace it

W
w
Worm

X-Ray Fish
is for
X-RAY
FISH
spell it
EX
letter X

Color It

XIPHIAS

Trace it

Yak

letter y

Trace it

Zebra

Z

is for - ZEBRA

Spell it

Zz

Z

z

zebu zebu